The Mystery Land

The Mystery Land

Amerindian Poems

Freely adapted by

William C. Tucker

Elk Heart Press

© William Canavan Tucker 2009

Elk Heart Press
116 Pinehurst Avenue, J-53
New York, New York 10033

This book is set in Garamond.

ISBN: 978-0-578-01376-3

Dedicated to the Memory of

Edgardo Alberto Vega Yunqué

INTRODUCTION

When I first began reading Amerindian "poetry," I was impressed by the unencumbered and robust, yet highly spiritual and reflective, even classical sensibility I found there. Yet the English renditions of ethnologists and other well-meaning but frequently uninspired translators often left much to be desired. Quite simply, in many cases I felt that I could do better--and that the unknown or long-departed Native authors of the works *deserved* better. That is not to say that we do not owe those ethnologists, some of whom were and are Native people themselves, an enormous debt of gratitude, since the written Amerindian literature we have is but a small fraction of the lost whole. Yet for these works to endure, they must not only be accessible to an English-speaking public, they must also be memorable: in other words, true and lasting poetry.

Although I found in what Native American anthologies there were a unique and visionary poetry, and much (which I've left alone) seemed quite self-sufficient, many of the works I most admired seemed to my ear to have become distorted in translation. It was as if I were looking through an opaque screen or fun-house mirror at a compelling image, the force of which, though not the detail, yet shone through. Often the Native poems had gone through several languages before arriving in English, and both the translations and versification, if any, seemed suspect. For example, many of the works in this book from Mesoamerica were first translated into Spanish many centuries ago, then found their way from Spanish to English by various routes, even though the original Mayan or Nahuatl texts have long existed and are now accessible. In addition, early post-Conquest translations of Mesoamerican works tended to import Christian concepts and metaphors often inconsistent with the meaning of the originals.

While the English variants often seemed forced, when I saw phonetic transcriptions of the Native originals, they seemed highly rhythmical, alliterative and melodic, as befits lyric poetry, that is, poetry intended to be sung. In order to restore (or rather, imagine) the highly formal, harmonious sound and rhythm of the unheard originals, I felt it was necessary to take liberties with what appeared through the English renditions to be their meaning, yet the very distance of the source in time and uncertainty of the route from Native tongue to English seemed to justify and almost to demand it.

There is a further rationale for my having freely interpreted these works in the fundamental, deep-rooted *individualism* of Native peoples. From this perspective, everyone is assumed to be a poet, just as once, up to fairly recent times on this side of the great ocean and in ancient times on the other, every man was expected to bear-- or be borne upon--a shield. I will just quote one authority for this individualistic quality, Smohalla, a visionary and spiritual leader of the Nez Percés who opposed assimilation:

"My young men will never work, for men who work cannot dream, and wisdom comes in dreams."

--- *American Indian Prose and Poetry*, Margot Astrov, ed., Capricorn Books, New York, 1962, p. 85

Therefore, I deem it proper to have thrust myself fully into these poems, much more as poet-dreamer than mere scribe, rejecting slavish conservation in an attempt to capture the sound, rhythm and spirit, if not the "letter," of the originals.

Of course, and this is where I tread with some trepidation, like all peoples Native Americans have their orthodoxies, and many of the sources for these poems are sacred texts passed down orally from ancient times, with many deep apologies for the slightest, inadvertent alteration, and often mortal fear of the consequences to an errant speaker. There are also songs in this book once considered the property of the author or society composing them, or their designees, the unauthorized use of which might seem infringement or outright theft. However, to the extent I may be seen as having pilfered or tampered with these texts, it should be remembered that I am not the first, nor have I done so in the native tongue, their natural and proper medium of transmission. Furthermore, I do not intend that they be used in any way other than to be read and understood as English poetry, not for healing, prayer, power, love, fertility or passing down of myth or sacred origins, or any other purpose for which they may have originally been intended other than as song. Many references in the originals, without a deep understanding of their meaning in the Native cultural and historical context, cannot and, I would venture, need not be fully understood by the contemporary reader in order to appreciate their value as literature.

I wish no one to be offended by my poor efforts. They have an ambitious purpose: to help bring to modern writing the sensibility and sound of this continent's ancient roots in orally-transmitted verse, which are or should be just as dear to all of us as Homer, *Arthur*, or the *Tain*, and springing from those roots and from this soil, the same towering designs and great capacity for deeds we all-too-often mourn as having been, but long-since passed away.

*   *   *

TABLE OF CONTENTS

I, the song,
I walk here.

--Modoc

The Mystery Land
(Aztec)

Ah, flowers in our hair!
Ah, songs we raise,
On our way to the
Mystery land!

If only for a day,
Traveling together,
Let us be companions
On that friendless road.

We must leave our
Blossoms and our songs
Behind, yet shall the Earth
Remain unchanged. Rejoice!

*   *   *

Rain Song
(Quechua)

My mother, she bore me,

Ah!

Within a dark raincloud,

Ah!

To weep with the rain,

Ah!

To brood with the cloud.

*   *   *

The Creation
(Uitoto)

In the beginning nothing existed
But an illusion, a phantasm.
Our Father touched it, he felt
About the edges of the Mystery.

Nothing else existed.

Then in a dream, our Father held
The illusion close to his body,
Embraced it and pondered long
And thought deeply upon it.

Nothing else existed.

Then he attached to it the wisp
Of a dream, and spit magic upon it:
Thus he held the Mystery
As by a thread of raw cotton.

Nothing else existed.

Then suddenly seizing the mirage,
He threw it down and stamped upon it
Violently, sitting down at last to rest
Upon his dreamed and flattened earth.

Nothing else existed.

The earth-phantasm was now his,
So he spat out the forests and lakes;
Then he lay down on his beautiful Earth
And pulled over it the robe of the sky.

*   *   *

War Song
(Pawnee)

Let us see, is this real?
Let us see, is this real,
This life I am living?

You omniscient gods,
Show me! Is this real,
This life I am living?

*   *   *

Warrior Song
(Crow)

Lasting only are the heavens and the earth.
Old age is hard. *Don't be afraid!*

*   *   *

War Song
(After the Chippewa)

From the South,
Come the geese.

From the North
Comes the cold.

From the West
Come the rains.

From the East
Comes the dawn.

I cast it away,
My body.

*   *   *

Spell to Banish Illness
(Iroquois)

You have no right to trouble me.
Depart! I am too strong for you.
You steal away through my nostrils,
You, who would devour me whole!

I grow stronger as you creep away.
A mighty power grows within me.
You can't subdue me, not for all
Your guile. I spit you out! *Depart!*

*   *   *

Warrior's Song
(Osage)

I am one who has
Made a god his body:
The god of Night
I have made my body;

Therefore, it is difficult
For Death to find me.

If you also make
That god your body,
The god of Night
To be your body,

Then you too shall be
Invisible to Death.

*   *   *

Song
(Eskimo)

As I recall my old adventures,
When by a shore wind I drifted out
In my kayak, and thought I was in
Peril, my fears so grand, my thoughts

On all those vital things I felt I had
To have, the great renown I longed for;
And yet, there is only one thing,
One great thing, the only thing:

To live to see from house and hill,
In resting and in purpose,
The great day that dawns anew,
The great light that fills the world!

*　　*　　*

Crier's Speech Before a Dance
(Nez Percés)

People!

Lay everything aside.
For now we are going
To have a dance.

People!

Get out your finest clothes,
And put them on; make
Ready for the dance.

People!

Now we shall see the
Raiment of our heroes,
The dead of long ago.

People!

Everyone must come,
Because another time
We may not be living.

*   *   *

Dance Song
(Ayacucho)

Wake up! Rise up, you dancers!
In the street, a dog howls. Death
Comes to all, but dance comes
Kicking too, and welcome both!

Comes the dance, one must dance.
Comes death, and all dance too.
May both be welcome here always.
Ah, what a wind! Ah, what a chill!

*   *   *

The Five Ages
(After the Aztec)

Our ancestors said there were four ages,
And this is the fifth. The first age
Was called the Age of Water, when
Everything was washed away, and

All the people turned to fish. The second
Age was called the Age of Cats, when
The sky cracked, the Sun tumbled from
Its course; when at midday darkness

Fell and jaguars ate human flesh. The third
Age was called the Age of Burning Rain,
When fire rained down upon the earth,
And those on whom it fell were burnt alive.

The fourth was called the Age of Wind,
When everything was swept away;
The seas rose up and claimed the land,
And mountains changed their shape.

The last age is now, the Age of Change.
Its sign is stain of blood upon the moon.
In it, the earth will quake, the sky will weep.
In it, will come plague and famine.

*　　*　　*

Love Song for the Dead
(Kwakiutl)

You are hard-hearted and cruel, my dear.
It is long since you left me so casually.
I am tired of waiting for you. I shall go
Down into the lower world to find you.

*   *   *

Lament of Age
(Teton Sioux)

I have been a wolf.
But now I hear the
Hooting of the owls,
And I fear the night.

*   *   *

Declaration to the Sun
(Teton Sioux)

Great Sun! I am about to send a voice
Across the waters, over all the hills and
Mountains of the Earth. Hear me! *Like
Fire I, too, shall endure!* There, it's done.

        *   *   *

Song for the New Moon
(After the Takelma)

I shall arise anew, even when
They say of me: he's gone.

Just as you, I shall emerge again,
Gleaming like an unsheathed blade.

Even when all forms of darkness
Eat you up, spirits, frogs and spells,

Still you rise again above the hills.
Just as you, shall I in time to come.

*   *   *

Formula to Destroy Injustice
(After the Cherokee)

Listen! I have come to end your days!
You are bloated and suffused with greed.
Your name is loathsome to all and hateful,
Your issue an abomination to the Earth.

I have come to cover you with the black soil
Of the prairie and the red dust of the mesas,
With the laughter of women and children
And the cold contempt of honest men.

Toward the land of shadows lies your way,
Well-paved; so shall you go; the grass leaps
Up to cover you; the sandy shore revolves;
The mountain peak stoops down to cover you.

Even the crows spit on you! With the heart's
Shroud I've come to wrap you up; deep under
Ground I bury you; I cover you with heavy slabs.
Your memory shall fade away forever! *Listen!*

*   *   *

Love Song
(After the Makah)

No matter how long
It's been, you always
Return to my thoughts.

Perhaps, reading this
Some day, you'll know
That I think of you still.

*　　*　　*

Woman's Complaint
    (Aztec)

What can I do?
He compares me
To a wild flower.

When I wither
In his hands, he'll
Cast me aside.

    *   *   *

To a Woman Loved
  (Otomi)

In the sky there's a moon;
On your face, a mouth.
In the sky are many stars,
On your face, just two eyes.

*   *   *

They Shall not Wither
(After the Aztec)

They shall not wither, my petals.
.   Nor shall they age, my songs.

I lift them by my feathered dreams;
I scatter them; they spread about.

Though on earth they may yellow
And fall, they shall be gathered by

The wind, and come to rest at last
In the sticky sanctuary of the heart.

*   *   *

Song of the Spirit
(Luiseño)

At the time of my death,
As I sensed it draw near,
I was surprised and sad:
I grieved to leave my home.

I have ranged far and wide, to
The north, south, east and west,
Seeking a way to escape death,
But have found no trail, no path.

*   *   *

Butterfly Song
(Acoma Pueblo)

Butterfly, butterfly, butterfly.
See it hover in the flowers,
Like a baby learning to walk.

*   *   *

My Breath
(Apache)

In the place called
Dawning with Life,
The Sky Gods came.
I went among them.

One spoke to me
Four times. He came
To me with a voice
Of thunder, four times.

He questioned me
Four times. Each
Time I answered him,
My breath became.

*　　*　　*

Spell Against Disease
(Maya)

Cursed be the Snake of creation,
The enemy of humankind alone.
Behead him! Cleave him! Claw him,
Gods of the Earth! Gods of the Sky!

Put an end to his machinations,
An end to his lust to devour us.
You Gods of the Earth, strike him!
Roughly hold and beat him!

You Gods of the Sky, swoop down
To snatch him up and crush him!
Curses upon him! Strip off his skin
And hang it up for all to see.

*   *   *

Song of the Sky Loom
(Tewa Pueblo)

O our Mother the Earth! O our Father the Sky!
Your children are we, and with bent backs
We bear you as gifts those things that you love;
Then weave us a radiant garment of gladness.

Let its warp be the white light of dawn;
Let its weft be the red light of dusk;
Let its fringe be of rain, blue and white;
Let its design be the rainbow triumphant.

Thus weave us a garment of radiant splendor,
That we may walk in adornment where birds sing,
That we may walk in adornment where grass grows.
O our Mother the Earth! O our Father the Sky!

*　*　*

Dawn Boy's Song
(Navajo)

In the house of long life, there I dwell.
In the house of happiness, there I dwell.

Beauty before me, with it I wander.
Beauty below me, with it I wander.

Beauty above me, with it I wander.
Beauty around me, with it I wander.

In old age traveling, with it I wander.
On a trail of beauty forever I wander.

*   *   *

The Sky
(Fox)

The sky, the sky,
Will weep, will weep.

At the end of the Earth,
The sky will weep.

*   *   *

We Spirits
(Wintu)

Down west, down west,
We dance, we dance,

We spirits, we spirits,
Weeping, we dance.

*   *   *

The Being Without a Face
(Iroquois)

Our grandfathers, long since departed,
In whom we trusted, our minds at rest,
Because they could not see its face--

The face of that Being that still abuses us
Day and night, that thing of darkness
Lying close by our homes in the shadows,

The Being that goes about menacingly with
Gory, uplifted blade, feverishly muttering
Its dread purpose: "I will destroy you all,

And break the circle of the tribes"--
Vowed to call it henceforth *Great Destroyer*,
Thing Malefic of Itself, The Being Without a Face.

*   *   *

Song of a Lovesick Man
     (Kwakiutl)

Whenever I eat,
     I taste the pain of your love.

Whenever I sleep,
     I dream the pain of your love.

Whatever I touch,
     I feel the pain of your love.

Wherever I walk,
     I bear the pain of your love.

                  *   *   *

Drinking Song
(Papago)

Dizzying amazement,
Great whirlwinds churn
Within my empty bowl,
Turned upside-down.

A great bear heart!
A great eagle heart!
A great hawk heart!
A great whirlwind!

All these have come
Together here within
My brimming bowl.
Now, *will you drink?*

*   *   *

Prayer
(Aztec)

Lord most benevolent and resourceful:
I implore you, make it your manifest will
That this People enjoy the goods and riches only
You can provide, as if plucked from emptiness,
Pleasant to the touch and savory to taste,
Delighting the senses and calming the mind,
Though passing but briefly, as if in a dream.

*   *   *

Wind Song
(Pima)

The voice of Wind is thunder;
    The breath of Wind is cloud.
Now Wind begins to sing;
    Now Wind begins to sing:

I go wandering over the hills;
    My thunder rolls over the valleys.
The land stretches away before me,
    Before me, it stretches away.

The stealthy Snake Wind comes,
    The Snake Wind comes singing:
Over the gusty mountains I creep,
    Through the distant mountain passes.

The Snake Wind comes to me.
    The black Snake Wind comes to me,
Comes and wraps itself about me,
    Whispering its songs.

*   *   *

Los Pochtecas
Chilam Balam
(Maya)

You are to wander,
Entering and departing
From strange villages,
Peddling your wares.

It may seem you will
Accomplish nothing.
It may be your work
Will not find favor,

But do not turn back.
Keep a firm step:
Something you will achieve.
Something will be given you.

*   *   *

Song of The Tree of the Great Peace
Degandawidah
(Iroquois)

If any man of any nation wishes to obey the laws
Of the Great Peace, let him follow the roots of
The Tree of the Great Peace to their source,

And he shall be welcome to shelter beneath it.
The smoke of the council fire of the Great Peace
Shall pierce the sky so all nations may find it.

I, Degandawidah, and the Chiefs of the Council
Here uproot the tallest pine, and into the cavity
Cast all weapons of war--those known and those

Yet unknown, straightforward ones and devious--
Into the heart of the Earth, close by those streams
Flowing deep underground, unseen and unheard,

Which nourish our mother the Earth, black streams
Flowing swiftly toward the dark, unknown regions,
Buried from sight forever under a righted Tree.

*   *   *

The Newly-Created World
(Winnebago)

Beautiful it was, this
Newly-created world.
Over its great floor
Our Mother the Earth
Spread her green cloak,
And the escaping odors
Were pleasant to inhale.

*   *   *

War Song
(Sioux)

Make way.
In a sacred
Manner

I come.
The earth
Is mine.

* * *

The Council that Led to War with the Nez Percés

Too-hul-hul-sote, General Howard recalled,
The one called by the whites *The Growler*,
Was chosen as speaker, and took up his theme.

The Earth was his mother, he said, she should
Not be disturbed by hoe or plow, post or fence.
Men should subsist on what grows of itself.

He spoke of the "chieftanship" of the Earth,
Which cannot be sold or given away. Surely
The white Long-knives must understand this?

He was answered. We do not wish to change
Your religion, they said, but you must speak
Of practical things. Twenty times over you say

The Earth is our mother, you say we have
Stewardship over the Earth. *Let us hear it
No more*, but come to the business at hand.

*   *   *

Song of the Fallen Deer
  (Pima/Papago)

Over there, I ran trembling;
Over here, I ran trembling,
The hunter, he pursued me
With bow and singing arrow.

On the grass, I staggered, the
Snapping bow made me dizzy.
On the mountain, I slipped, the
Humming arrow made me dizzy.

The hunter, he caught me,
Cut and threw my horns away.
The hunter, he killed me,
Cut and threw my feet away.

Now the flies are sated;
They fall fluttering to earth.
The drunken butterflies sit
With opening and closing wings.

*   *   *

Prayer to the Sun
(After the Havasupai)

Sun, grandfather, shine forth again
Upon the Earth; do us a great good
By your mere presence, your smiling
Countenance beaming on us always.

Beneath the spinning sky you never
Rest, but only lie to rise at once on
Some far plain, lifting ever to excite
And render fruitful all the Earth.

Sun, grandfather, who impregnates all
The valleys, potent and omniscient Sun,
My prayer is this: let me always, and
Forever, burn bright as you do now.

*   *   *

A Song of Nezahualcoyotl
(Nahuatl)

The riches of this world are only lent us.
The things we so enjoy are not our own.
The sun pours down its gold upon us;
Waterfalls bequeath rich fountains to us;

Colors touch us like the shimmering fingers
Of *quetzal* wings. Yet none of this can we own
For more than a day; none of these beautiful
Things can we keep for more than an hour!

One thing alone can we own forever:
The memory of right, the sweet remembrance
Of one good act or one just man--this alone
Can never be taken away, will never die.

*   *   *

Medicine Song
(Pima)

The yellow wren herself pulled out
Her feathers, and with them made me
A prostitute, a whore running about
The land, yellow feathers in her hair.

Blue bird drifting at the edge of the land,
Gliding on a blue wind, in a blue cloud,
White wind swirling around, blowing dust:
You birds will see. You winds will see.

Moons are shining in my belly here.
You men will see. You women will see.
The distant Moon shall come to me,
When I play upon my melancholy flute.

*   *   *

Gila Monster Song
(Pima)

Pitiable prostitute though I am,
My heart flowers with evening.
Whore! My heart flowers.

Around those two stones there,
Comes a black wind roaring, driving
The birds back and forth, fluttering.

On the top of that white rock there,
Under blue clouds, frogs are singing--
So many, so many together singing!

*   *   *

Elegy Dream Song
(Papago)

In the great Night my heart will go out.
Darkness will come creeping toward me.
With a sound like the sound of a rattle,
In the great Night my heart will go out.

I am running now toward a mountain
Range; from its ancient, snowy peaks
I'll see the white dawn-light. I die and
Lie dead here. I die and lie dead here!

*   *   *

A Fragment
(Maya)

Wise is the one
Who meditates on

The goodness of all
That exists in the sky,

On the earth, in the lakes,
And in the deep ocean.

*   *   *

Love-charm Song
(Tupi)

You magic power in the skies
Who gives the rains, make it
So that he, no matter how many

Women he has, will think them
All plain, remembering me when
The red sun droops in the west.

New moon, new moon: here am
I in your presence; make it so that
Only I may occupy his heart.

*   *   *

The North Star
  (Osage)

Then up sprang
A blazing star

From the Earth
Into the sky,

Where it stood
In all its beauty,

Pleasing
To look upon.

*   *   *

Tall Dog Tale
(Melecite)

There once was a woman who
Admired a dog: she thought the dog
Was handsome and she liked his face.
That night the dog turned into
A man and became her husband.
"Never tell anyone I used to be
A dog," he whispered to his wife,
"Never mention it at all." For a
Long time they lived together.
She never thought of him as a dog.
She never spoke of it, not once.
But one day she saw some dogs
In the village, all chasing a bitch
Everywhere, here and there,
And without thinking she asked
Her husband if he would like to be
One of them again, and right away
He said yes, and turned back into
A dog and ran away with the others.

*   *   *

Guardian Spirit Song
(Nez Percés)

Ravening Coyote comes:
Red hands, red mouth,
Necklace of eyeballs.

*　　*　　*

Spring Song (fragment)
(Eskimo)

Glorious it is,

To see the young women in little
Groups, paying their visits to the
Houses. All at once, the men
Want so much to seem manly!

Glorious it is,

To see the long-haired caribou
Returning to their winter forests,
Following the ebb-mark of the tide
With storms of clattering hooves!

*   *   *

Tezozomoc
A Song of Nezahualcoyotl
(Nahuatl)

Listen! I, the singer, Nezahualcoyotl lament
The brevity of all life, and the brief time of even
My own powers. O restless and striving man,
When your death shall come, your world shall
Tumble into darkness and oblivion! The palaces and
Gardens of that great conqueror, that great king,
Tezozomoc, surely, one thought, would last
Forever, but now stand already sere and ruined.

All life at last is just illusion and betrayal.

Sorrowful and strange it is to reflect upon
The great Tezozomoc: watered by ambition,
He grew like a willow rising high above the
Saplings of the spring, rejoicing in long life and
Strength, until at last the storm winds of death
Tore him, even him, from his deep roots and
Dashed him in splinters to the ground. Now,
He is forever vanquished, withered and decayed,

All life at last is just illusion and betrayal.

None seeing this can keep from tears, from
Weeping; that these blossoms, these rich colors,
This rich life itself, are only petals blown on
The wind, that wither and fade in a moment.
You children of a strong people, ponder this!
Let the birds with their songs enjoy, while
They may, this house of flowery delights; let
The butterflies sip the nectar of its blooms.

*   *   *

Introduction of a Child

(Omaha)

Ho! You Sun, Moon, Stars, all you
That move in the heavens: hear me!
Into your midst has come a new life.
Consent, I implore you, consent!

Make its path smooth, that it may
Reach the brow of the first hill.

Ho! You Winds, Clouds, Rain, Mist,
All you that move in the air: hear me!
Into your midst has come a new life.
Consent, I implore you, consent!

Make its path smooth, that it may
Reach the brow of the second hill.

Ho! You Hills, Valleys, Rivers, Lakes,
Trees, all you of the earth: hear me!
Into your midst has come a new life.
Consent, I implore you, consent!

Make its path smooth, that it may
Reach the brow of the third hill.

Ho! You birds, big and small, you
Insects, you forest animals: hear me!
Into your midst has come a new life.
Consent, I implore you, consent!

Make its path smooth, that it may
Reach the brow of the fourth hill.

Ho! All you of the heavens, all you
Of the air, all you of the earth: hear me!
Into your midst has come a new life.
Consent, I implore you, consent!

Make its path smooth, that it may
Travel beyond the four hills.

*   *   *

The Rock
(Omaha)

Unmoved and unmoving
From time without beginning,
You rest there, in the midst
Of the path, in the midst
Of the winds, in the midst
Of the rain.
        You rest
Covered with droppings,
Grass springing up between
Your toes, your head bedecked
With the down of birds.
From time immemorial,
You wait, Aged One.

    *   *   *

From the Aztec Calendar:
The First Month
(Nahuatl)

In the rites of the first month
They slew many children. They
Sacrificed them in different holy
Places on the mountain tops,

Tearing their hearts from them
In honor of the gods of water,
So that these might give rain.
Many captives were slain also.

The children were decked in rich
Finery when they were taken to be
Killed. They were carried in litters
Upon the shoulders of the people.

The litters were adorned with bright
Feathers and flowers, and the priests
Went before them, playing upon
Instruments, dancing and singing.

If the children wept or shed tears,
Those who carried them rejoiced,
For it was an omen that there
Would be much rain that year.

*   *   *

Song of Lamentation
(Aztec)

Weeping, I, the singer, weave of my tears
A solemn shroud of whispered song;
I call to mind the bits and shards of youths
Gone early to the dark, obsidian plain,

Once beautiful and noble here on earth,
Now dried and withered like discarded
Petals, split to fragments like an emerald,
And with the full complicity of their Creator!

Alas! I sing in grief for those lost children.
Would that I could turn and grasp their
Hands once more. Would that I could call
Them back from that dark land to walk

Again on earth, that they and we might sing
In praise and for the pleasure of the Cause
Of All: could they ever blame or be
Ungrateful to Him, who gave them life?

I weep therefore in my heart as I, the singer
Here recall my memories of grievous harms
Both cold and unavenged. Would that
They could hear me in that darkened land,

Were only I to sing some worthy song! Would
That I could gladden them, console them
In their torments and their endless sufferings!
But how can such a thing be done?

From what deep well to draw that healing
Balm? I cannot touch, nor can I soothe them
With my guileful artifice of sound and sense
As one may, eye to eye, on this our gentle Earth.

*   *   *

Song of the Earth Spirit
Origin Legend
(Navajo)

I, I am the spirit within the Earth.
It is lovely indeed; it is lovely indeed.

The feet of the Earth are my feet.
The legs of the Earth are my legs.

The strength of the Earth is my strength.
The thoughts of the Earth are my thoughts.

The voice of the Earth is my voice.
All that belongs to the Earth belongs

Also to me; all that surrounds
The Earth also surrounds me.

I, I am the sacred words of the Earth.
It is lovely indeed; it is lovely indeed.

*   *   *

Twelfth Song of the Thunder
(Navajo)

The voice that beautifies the land,
The voice above, the voice of thunder
Within the dark cloud, again and again
It sounds, the voice that beautifies the land.

The voice that beautifies the land,
The voice below, the grasshopper's voice
Among the reeds, again and again
It sounds, the voice that beautifies the land.

*   *   *

From the Wind Chant
(Navajo)

The patient was twice-bathed, sacredly.
Then, his body was painted with the sun
On his breast and the wind above, the
Moon on his back, arrows on his arms,

Snakes on his legs, and on each shoulder,
A white cross. To his head they tied
A prayer plume and they painted his face
White on the forehead, red across the eyes,

And yellow on the chin. They mixed herbs,
And Blue Jay came, and the Whirling Winds.
The singer stroked the patient's body,
And pressed his body to the patient's body.

"Have you learned?" he was asked, and he said
"Yes." They sang all night and he learned and
Was well. Then he was told to remember it all,
For what is forgotten goes back to the gods.

*　　*　　*

Love Charm Song
(Chippewa)

I can charm that man, I'll make
Him think of nothing else but me.
He'll become entranced by me:

What are you saying to me,
That I am dressed in the colors
Of the roses, and as beautiful?

 I'll charm him into shyness:
What can be the matter with him,
That he is so bashful with me?

I'll addle him wherever he may go:
Beyond the furthest northern sea,
Or in the very center of the earth!

*   *   *

From the Aztec Calendar:
The Seventh Month
(Nahuatl)

In the feast of the seventh month
Was slain the Woman in the likeness

Of the goddess Uixtociuatl, Tlaloc's
Sister. Women, old and young, and

Girls, wearing garlands and holding
Flowers, dancing and singing, led the

Captives and the Woman to Tlaloc's
Temple, where the priests slew first

The captives, then the Woman in
The golden likeness of the goddess.

*   *   *

Aztec Song
(Nahuatl)

We only came to sleep awhile.
We only came to dream awhile.
It can't be true, no, it can't be true
That we came to truly *live* on earth.

We are like the new, spring grass;
Our hearts have grown green again
And put out shoots; yet like the rose,
We blossom just to wither on this earth.

*   *   *

Magpie Song
(Navajo)

The magpie! The magpie!
In the white tips of its wings
Are the footsteps of morning.
It dawns! It dawns!

*   *   *

Offering
(Zuñi)

That our mother the Earth may be
Clothed in a robe of white cornmeal;

That she may be adorned with flowers;
That on yonder mossy mountain top

The trees may huddle together with cold,
Their arms broken by heavy drifts;

So that the land may be thus, I have
Made my prayers into living beings.

*   *   *

A Song of Nezahualcoyotl
(Nahuatl)

The fleeting pomps of this world are like
The green willow tree, which, aspiring to
Greatness, is yet consumed by fire, falls
To the ax, or lies uprooted by the wind.

The grandeurs of life are like the flowers
In color and in fate: their beauty remains
Only so long as their chaste, fingered buds
Can pluck the dewy pearls of the dawn.

But scarcely has the Cause of All directed
Upon them the rich rays of the Sun, when
Their beauty and glory fail, and the brilliant
Colors of their youth wither and fade.

The realms of flowers count their fragrant
Dynasties by hours: those which at morning
Reigned in beauty, by evening weep for the
Destruction of their thrones, and for the fate

That drove them to such loss, to destitution
And the grave. All things of earth must
Find an end, and in the midst of joyous life,
The breath fails, one sinks to the ground.

All Earth is a grave, and nothing escapes it.
Nothing is so perfect that it cannot age.
The rivers, brooks, and waterfalls flow on,
Never to return to their beginnings.

That which was yesterday is not today;
And trust not what is today to be tomorrow.
The caverns of the earth are filled with
Pestilential dust which once was bone and

Flesh of those who sat in judgment upon thrones,
Decided causes, ruled assemblies, led conquering
Hosts, gained treasure, razed and trampled
Temples, all in pride, in majesty and pomp.

Ha! Were I to take you into the obscure bowels
Of this temple, and ask you which bones were
Those of the great Achalchiuhtlanextin of the Toltecs,
Which those of the devout Necaxecmitl, worshipper

Of the gods; if I ask where lies now the peerless beauty
Of the glorious empress Xiuhtzal, where lie the sacred
Ashes of our first father, Xolotl, or the beneficent
Nopal, even the still-warm cinders of my own father,

The unhappy and luckless Ixtlilxochitl, if I continued
Questioning you thus concerning our august ancestors,
What would you reply? The same as I: *I know not,*
For first and last are all confounded in the common clay.

Their fate shall be ours, and that of all who
Follow us. Unconquered princes! Warlike chiefs!
Let us yet seek and sigh for the next world
Where all is eternal, nothing is corruptible.

The darkness of the sepulcher is but the
Chamber of the glorious Sun, and the obscure
Night but serves to grace the brilliant stars.
No one has the power to change these ancient

Lights, from which shines forth their Maker's
Countenance; and as we see them now,
So did our ancestors from earliest times,
And so shall our posterity, down to the last.

*   *   *

Hear My Voice
(Cherokee)

Hear my voice, you birds of war!
I'll soon prepare a feast for you.
As you fly over the ranks of the
Enemy, like you I'll fly there too.

Give me the swiftness of your wings;
Give me the vengeance of your claws;
Give me the strong arms of my friends,
I'll fly straight to the enemy's heart!

*   *   *

Omen
(Aztec)

By day, fire came raining down.
Three stars together fell to earth,

Their long tails extending in
A storm of spark and flame.

Out of the West they came,
Traveling toward the East.

The people saw and screamed with
A sound like the shaking of bells.

*   *   *

Coyote Tale
(Hopi)

A long time ago a beautiful girl
Lived in the village of old Oraibi.
All the young men wanted to marry her,
But she refused them all.

The young men all gave her flowers.
Some even went long distances
To find rare ones for her,
But she refused them all.

Far away in the north country
Yellow Cloud Chief heard of her.
He made a beautiful bridal gown for her:
Two robes, beaded moccasins, a silver belt.

He came to the village and offered
Them to her, but she refused.
Then Blue Cloud Chief of the west
Offered her a bridal gown of blue.

Red Cloud Chief of the south
Offered her a bridal gown of red.
White Cloud Chief of the east
Offered her a bridal gown of white.

Black Cloud Chief from above
Offered her a bridal gown of black.
Grey Cloud Chief from below, a gown
Of grey. But she refused them all.

Now far away in the south the rain god
Pavayoykashi heard of her beauty.
He painted himself and dressed
Like the flute players, the dancers--

Like a Kachina, with a black line across
His painted face, and a bow and arrows
In a beaded quiver of panther skin.
He went to her adorned like that,

And she liked him and promised
To speak to her parents about him.
Now at that time Old Man Coyote
Lived just west of the village

In the place called Coyote Gap today.
Secretly Coyote went to the house
Of Pavayoykashi, and stole his costume
And ornaments. Dressed and painted

Like Pavayoykashi he went to the girl
And deceived her, looking like her lover,
And willingly she went with Old Man Coyote
To his house and bed, just by the village.

Pavayoykashi, his costume and ornaments stolen,
Followed the tracks of the thief to the house
Of the girl, and from there to Coyote's house.
All the young men wanted to kill Old Man Coyote,

Enraged that Coyote had stolen the beauty who
Had refused them all, but Coyote escaped and ran
To the mesa west of the village, and safe on the mesa
He shouted back in derision and shook the genitals

With which he had enjoyed their beautiful maiden.
Then he disappeared, running away across the mesa.
Now Pavayoykashi, seeing this, brought a great storm
With wind and rain and thunder, and hid himself

In the thunder. He rode the storm far and wide,
Looking for Old Man Coyote, and when he found him
Walking on the mesa, with a shout of thunder
Struck him dead with lightening from the storm.

*   *   *

You Say
Smohalla
(Nez Percés)

You say to plow is best,
But shall I take a knife
And cut my mother's breast?

You ask me to dig stone,
But shall I reach beneath
My mother's skin for bone?

You say cut hay, but dare
I, for a silver coin,
Cut off my mother's hair?

*   *   *

Prayer for the Day
(Nootka)

You, whose day this is, who dreams
The day: make it delightful. Take out
Your rainbow tints, your brush of fire,
And paint this day to make it beautiful.

＊　　＊　　＊

NOTES ON THE POEMS

I, THE SONG (Modoc) (p. 1): From *The Magic World; American Indian Songs and Poems*, William Brandon, ed., Ohio Univ. Press, 1991, p. 3; from a translation in A. I. Kroeber, "Handbook of California Indians," Bureau of American Ethnology, *Bulletin 78*, Washington D.C., 1925.

THE MYSTERY LAND (Aztec) (p. 2): From *In the Trail of the Wind, American Indian Poems and Ritual Orations*, John Bierhorst, ed., p. 101; translated from the Aztec by Angel Garibay, in his *La Literatura de los Aztecas*, 1964, p. 57; translated by Bierhorst from the Spanish.

RAIN SONG (Quechua) (p. 3): From *In the Trail of the Wind, American Indian Poems and Ritual Orations*, John Bierhorst, ed., p. 123; translated from the Quechua into French by R. and M. d'Harcourt, in their *La Musique des Incas*, 1925, p. 368, and from French into English by Bierhorst.

THE CREATION (Uitoto) (p. 4): From *American Indian Prose and Poetry*, Margot Astrov, ed., Capricorn Books, New York, 1962, p. 325; translated from K.T. Preuss, *Die Religion und Mythologie der Uitoto*, pp. 166.

WAR SONG (Pawnee) (p. 6): From *American Indian Prose and Poetry*, Margot Astrov, ed., Capricorn Books, New York, 1962, p. 109; attributed to Daniel G. Brinton, *Essays of an Americanist*, p. 292. According to Brinton, this is sung "when a warrior goes out all alone on the warpath from which it is likely he will never return."

WARRIOR SONG (Crow) (p. 7): From *American Indian Prose and Poetry*, Margot Astrov, ed., Capricorn Books, New York, 1962, p. 90; attributed to Robert H. Lowie, *The Religion of the Crow Indians*, p. 417. (It is worth noting that, according to Astrov, this poem was the possession of a man called "The Warrior-Wants-to-Die," who once addressed a group of youths about to go on the warpath, in part, as follows: "When a woman gives birth, it takes her a long time and she does not know whether she will live or not. *You* have it easy.")

WAR SONG (Chippewa) (p. 8): Freely adapted from *The Sky Clears, Poetry of the American Indians*, A. Grove Day, ed., p. 156; attributed to Henry Rowe Schoolcraft, *Historical and Statistical Information Respecting the History, Condition, and Prospects of the Indian Tribes of the Untied States*, 6 vols., Philadelphia, 1851-1857.

SPELL TO BANISH ILLNESS (Iroquois) (p. 9): From *In the Trail of the Wind, American Indian Poems and Ritual Orations*, John Bierhorst, ed., p. 163; translated from the Iroquois by A.C. Parker, published in *36ᵗʰ Annual Archaeological Report, being part of Appendix to the Report of the Minister of Education*, Ontario, 1928, p. 14.

WARRIOR'S SONG (Osage) (p. 10): From *American Indian Prose and Poetry*, Margot Astrov, ed., Capricorn Books, New York, 1962, p. 102 (a fragment from "A Warrior's Songs from the Mourning Rite"); attributed to Francis LaFlesche, *The War Ceremony of the Osage Indians*, pp. 123-4. LaFlesche, an Omaha and ethnologist, began his career working with Alice Fletcher during her visit to the Omahas in 1883. Her "The 'Wawan' or Pipe Dances of the Omahas," published in 1884, resulted from that trip. *The Sky Clears, Poetry of the American Indians*, A. Grove Day, ed., p. 29.

SONG (Eskimo) (p. 11): From *In the Trail of the Wind, American Indian Poems and Ritual Orations*, John Bierhorst, ed., p. 164; translated from the Eskimo by Knud Rasmussen, in his *Intellectual Culture of the Copper Eskimo* (translated from Rasmussen's Danish into English by W.E. Calvert), 1932, p. 53.

CRIER'S SPEECH BEFORE A DANCE (Nez Percés) (p. 12): From *American Indian Prose and Poetry*, Margot Astrov, ed., Capricorn Books, New York, 1962, p. 88; taken by Astrov from *Folk-Tales of Salishan and Sahaptin Tribes*, Herbert J. Spinden, Franz Boaz, ed., p. 201.

DANCE SONG (Ayacucho) (p. 13): From *American Indian Prose and Poetry*, Margot Astrov, ed., Capricorn Books, New York, 1962, p. 344; attributed to R. et M. d'Harcourt, *La musique des Incas et ses survivances*, p. 477.

THE FIVE AGES (Aztec) (p. 14): From *In the Trail of the Wind, American Indian Poems and Ritual Orations*, John Bierhorst, ed., pp. 6-7; translated from the Aztec by Miguel León-Portilla, in his *Pre-Columbian Literatures of Mexico*, 1969, U. of Oklahoma Press, pp. 35-7.

LOVE SONG FOR THE DEAD (Kwakiutl) (p. 15): From *American Indian Prose and Poetry*, Margot Astrov, ed., Capricorn Books, New York, 1962, p. 280;

attributed to Franz Boaz, "The Ethnology of the Kwakiutl," *35th Annual Report*, Bureau of American Ethnology, Washington, D.C., 1921, p. 1306; also appears in *The Sky Clears, Poetry of the American Indians*, A. Grove Day, ed., p. 54, with attribution to the same source.

LAMENT OF AGE (Teton Sioux) (p. 16): From *American Indian Prose and Poetry*, Margot Astrov, ed., Capricorn Books, New York, 1962, p. 126 ("Song of Failure"); attributed to Frances Densmore, *Teton Sioux Music*, p. 339.

DECLARATION TO THE SUN (Teton Sioux) (p. 17): From *American Indian Prose and Poetry*, Margot Astrov, ed., Capricorn Books, New York, 1962, p. 123; attributed to Frances Densmore, *Teton Sioux Music*, p. 184. The opening prayer of the Sun Dance, given by Astrov economically as:

Grandfather!
A voice I am going to send.
Hear me!
All over the universe
A voice I am going to send.
Hear me,
Grandfather!
I will live!
I have said it.

SONG FOR THE NEW MOON (Takelma) (p. 18): From *American Indian Prose and Poetry*, Margot Astrov, ed., Capricorn Books, New York, 1962, p. 277; attributed to Edward Sapir, *Takelma Texts*, p. 197.

FORMULA TO DESTROY INJUSTICE (Cherokee) (p. 19): Freely adapted from *American Indian Prose and Poetry*, Margot Astrov, ed., Capricorn Books, New York, 1962, p. 178; attributed to James Mooney, "The Sacred Formulas of the Cherokees," *7th Annual BAE Report*, Washington, D.C., 1891, p. 391 (originally titled "Formula to Destroy Life," intended to cause the death of an enemy). A different adaptation entitled "A Spell to Destroy Life," appears in *The Magic World; American Indian Songs and Poems*, William Brandon, ed., Ohio Univ. Press, 1991, p. 111, with the same attribution.

LOVE SONG (Makah) (p. 20): From *American Indian Prose and Poetry*, Margot Astrov, ed., Capricorn Books, New York, 1962, p. 278; attributed to Frances Densmore, "Nootka and Quileute Music," *BAE Bulletin 124*, 1939, p. 327-8; also appears in *In the Trail of the Wind, American Indian Poems and Ritual Orations*, John Bierhorst, ed., p. 78.

WOMAN'S COMPLAINT (Aztec) (p. 21): From *In the Trail of the Wind, American Indian Poems and Ritual Orations*, John Bierhorst, ed., p. 82; translated from the Aztec by Miguel León-Portilla, in his *Pre-Columbian Literatures of Mexico*, 1969, U. of Oklahoma Press, pp. 114-5.

TO A WOMAN LOVED (Otomi) (p. 22): From *In the Trail of the Wind, American Indian Poems and Ritual Orations*, John Bierhorst, ed., p. 75; translated from the Otomi by Angel Garibay, in his *Historia de la Literatura Náhuatl*, I, p. 239. The English version relied on by Bierhorst is by Miguel León-Portilla, after the Spanish of Garibay, in his *Pre-Columbian Literatures of Mexico*, 1969, U. of Oklahoma Press, p. 95.

THEY SHALL NOT WITHER (Aztec) (p. 23): From *In the Trail of the Wind, American Indian Poems and Ritual Orations*, John Bierhorst, Ed., p. 168; translated from the Aztec by Miguel León-Portilla, in his *Pre-Columbian Literatures of Mexico*, 1969, U. of Oklahoma Press, p. 89.

SONG OF THE SPIRIT (Luiseño) (p. 24): From *American Indian Prose and Poetry*, Margot Astrov, ed., Capricorn Books, New York, 1962, p. 262; attributed to Constance G. DuBois, *The Religion of the Luiseño Indians*, p. 110 (from the Quiot story).

BUTTERFLY SONG (Acoma Pueblo) (p. 25): From *In the Trail of the Wind, American Indian Poems and Ritual Orations*, John Bierhorst, ed., p. 110; translated from the Keresan, in Frances Densmore's "Music of Acoma, Isleta, Cochiti and Zuñi Pueblos," *BAE Bulletin* 165, 1957, p. 38.

MY BREATH (Apache) (p. 26): From *In the Trail of the Wind, American Indian Poems and Ritual Orations*, John Bierhorst, ed., p. 109; translated from the Apache by Pliny Goddard, in *Holmes Anniversary Volume*, 1916, pp. 134-5.

SPELL AGAINST DISEASE (Maya) (p. 27): From *In the Trail of the Wind, American Indian Poems and Ritual Orations*, John Bierhorst, ed., p. 151; translated from the Maya by Ralph Roys, in his *Ritual of the Bacabs*, Univ. of Oklahoma Press, 1965, pp. 46-7, and in his *The Book of Chilam Balam of Chumayel*, 1933, p. 99, fn. 3, 4.

SONG OF THE SKY LOOM (Tewa Pueblo) (p. 28): From *American Indian Prose and Poetry*, Margot Astrov, ed., Capricorn Books, New York, 1962, p. 221; attributed to Herbert J. Spinden, *Songs of the Tewa*, New York, 1933, p. 94; a different version appears in *The Magic World; American Indian Songs and Poems*, William Brandon, ed., Ohio Univ. Press, 1991, p. 49.

DAWN BOY'S SONG (Navajo) (p. 29): Vinson Brown, *Voices of Earth and Sky*, Stackpole Books, Harrisburg, Pennsylvania, 1974, p. 47; from "Navajo Myths, Prayers and Songs with Texts and Translations," Univ. of Cal. *Publications in American Archeaology and Ethnology*, Vol. 5, No. 2, Berkeley, 1907; republished in *Navajo Wildlands*, Ballantine Books-Sierra Club, San Francisco, 1969.

THE SKY (Fox) (p. 30): A fragment from *American Indian Prose and Poetry*, Margot Astrov, ed., Capricorn Books, New York, 1962, p. 152; attributed to Truman Michelson, *The Owl Sacred Pack of the Fox Indians*, p. 29; appears in a different form in *In the Trail of the Wind, American Indian Poems and Ritual Orations*, John Bierhorst, ed., p. 97, also attributed to Michelson, *Bureau of American Ethnology, Bulletin 72*, 1921, p. 29.

WE SPIRITS (Wintu) (p. 31): From *In the Trail of the Wind, American Indian Poems and Ritual Orations*, John Bierhorst, ed., p. 95; translated from the Wintu by D. Demetracopoulou, in his "Wintu Songs," *Anthropos*, vol. 30, 1935, p. 487.

THE BEING WITHOUT A FACE (Iroquois) (p. 32): From *In the Trail of the Wind, American Indian Poems and Ritual Orations*, John Bierhorst, ed., p. 89; translated from the Iroquois by J.N.B. Hewitt (ed. W. Fenton), in *Journal of the Washington Academy of Sciences*, Mar. 15, 1944, p. 75. "Circle of the tribes" as used here is meant to refer to the League of the Iroquois.

SONG OF A LOVESICK MAN (Kwakiutl) (p. 33): From *In the Trail of the Wind, American Indian Poems and Ritual Orations*, John Bierhorst, ed., p. 84; translated from the Kwakiutl by Franz Boas, in his *Kwakiutl Ethnography* (ed. Helen Codere), 1966, p. 348.

DRINKING SONG (Papago) (p. 34): From *In the Trail of the Wind, American Indian Poems and Ritual Orations*, John Bierhorst, ed., p. 64; translated from the Papago by Ruth Underhill, in her *Singing for Power*, 1938, p. 97.

PRAYER (Aztec) (p. 35): From *In the Trail of the Wind, American Indian Poems and Ritual Orations*, John Bierhorst, ed., p. 30; freely translated from the Aztec by Bernardino de Sahagún, in his *Historia General de las Cosas de Nueva España*, Libro 6, capítulo 2.; translated from the Spanish by Bierhorst.

WIND SONG (Pima) (p. 36): From *In the Trail of the Wind, American Indian Poems and Ritual Orations*, John Bierhorst, ed., p. 22; also appears in *The Sky Clears, Poetry of the American Indians*, A. Grove Day, ed., p. 88; translated from the Pima by Frank Russell, in his "The Pima Indians," *Bureau of American Ethnology, 26th Annual Report*, 1908, p. 324; a "medicine" or curing song.

LOS POCHTECAS, Chilam Balam (Maya) (p. 37): From Vinson Brown, *Voices of Earth and Sky*, Stackpole Books, Harrisburg, Pennsylvania, 1974, p. 103; taken from Irene Nicholson, *Mexican and Central American Mythology*, Hamilyn Publishing Group, 1967, p. 93; a poem of Chilam Balam, the great Mayan priest, poet and seer.

SONG OF THE TREE OF THE GREAT PEACE (Degandawidah) (Iroquois) (p. 38): From *The Magic World; American Indian Songs and Poems*, William Brandon, ed., Ohio Univ. Press, 1991, p. 102; adapted from William N. Fenton, ed., *Parker on the Iroquois*, Syracuse, 1968.

THE NEWLY-CREATED WORLD (Winnebago) (p. 39): From *In the Trail of the Wind, American Indian Poems and Ritual Orations*, John Bierhorst, ed., p. 5: translated from the Winnebago by Paul Radin, in his *The Road of Life and Death*, 1945, p. 254. Bierhorst notes possible missionary influences in this poem (from *Genesis*).

WAR SONG (Sioux) (p. 40): From *In the Trail of the Wind, American Indian Poems and Ritual Orations*, John Bierhorst, ed., p. 62; translated from the Sioux by Frances Densmore and Robert P. Higheagle, in Densmore's "Teton Sioux Music," *BAE Bulletin* 61, 1918, p. 351.

THE COUNCIL THAT LEAD TO WAR WITH THE NEZ PERCÉS (p. 41): From *The Portable North American Indian Reader*, Frederick Turner, ed., Penquin Books, New York, 1977, p. 232.

SONG OF THE FALLEN DEER (Pima/Papago) (p. 42): An amalgam of three works, the first of which is a Pima "hunting song," from *The Magic World; American Indian Songs and Poems*, William Brandon, ed., Ohio Univ. Press, 1991, p. 40, adapted by Brandon from the literal translation in Frank Russell, "The Pima Indians," *Twenty-sixth Annual BAE Report*, Washington, D.C., pp. 299-300; different versions of this poem appear in *In the Trail of the Wind, American Indian Poems and Ritual Orations*, John Bierhorst, ed., p. 57, and *The Sky Clears, Poetry of the American Indians*, A. Grove Day, ed., p. 88, also attributed to Russell. The intoxication (dizziness, drunkenness, etc.) in this Pima song is caused by eating "thornapple," "jimson weed," or "Datura" leaves, depending on the translation. A second source is the Pima "Black-Tailed Deer Song," Bierhorst, p. 54, attributed to Russell, p. 317. The third source is a Papago "Song of the Deer," from Bierhorst's *Trail of the Wind.*, p. 56, translated from the Papago by Ruth Underhill, in her *Singing for Power*, 1938, pp. 58-9. The dizziness of the deer in this third poem is caused not by a drug, but by the "snapping bow" and "humming arrow."

PRAYER TO THE SUN (Havasupai) (p. 43): Freely adapted from *American Indian Prose and Poetry*, Margot Astrov, ed., Capricorn Books, New York, 1962, p. 30, a literal translation from Leslie Spier, *Havasupai Ethnography*, p. 286.

A SONG OF NEZALHUALCOYOTL (Nahuatl) (p. 44): From *The Magic World; American Indian Songs and Poems*, William Brandon, ed., Ohio Univ. Press, 1991, p. 26; adapted by Brandon from a translation by Fanny Calderon for William H. Prescott, appearing in a Note to his *Conquest of Mexico*. For comparison, this is Brandon's version:

A Song of Nezalhualcoyotl

The riches of this world are only lent us
The things that are so good to enjoy we do not own

The sun pours down gold
Fountains pour out green water
Colors touch us like fingers
Of green quetzal wings

None of this can we own for more than a day
None of these beautiful things can we keep for more than an hour

One thing along we can own forever
The memory of the just
The remembrance of a good act
The good remembrance of a just man

This one thing alone will never be taken away from us
Will never die

MEDICINE SONG (Pima) (p. 45): From *The Magic World; American Indian Songs and Poems*, William Brandon, ed., Ohio Univ. Press, 1991, p. 39; adapted by Brandon from the literal translation in Frank Russell, "The Pima Indians," *Twenty-sixth Annual BAE Report*, Washington, D.C., 1908. For comparison, this is Brandon's version:

PIMA: Medicine Song (Fragment)

The yellow wren himself pulled out his feathers
With them he made me a prostitute
A whore running over the land
With feathers on my head
With my hands clasped

Blue Bird drifted at the edge of the land
Lying on the blue wind

White Wind ran in wind
Blowing dust

Moons are shining in me here
You men will see
                    you women will see
The far distant moon come to meet me
When I blow upon this blue reed

GILA MONSTER SONG (Pima) (p. 46): From *The Magic World; American Indian Songs and Poems*, William Brandon, ed., Ohio Univ. Press, 1991, p. 38; adapted by Brandon from the literal translation in Frank Russell, "The Pima Indians," *Twenty-sixth Annual BAE Report*, Washington, D.C.

ELEGY DREAM SONG (Papago) (p. 47): From *The Magic World; American Indian Songs and Poems*, William Brandon, ed., Ohio Univ. Press, 1991, p. 42; appears in another form in *American Indian Prose and Poetry*, Margot Astrov, ed., Capricorn Books, New York, 1962, p. 196; attributed to Frances Densmore, "Papago Music," *BAE Bulletin 90*, Washington, D.C., 1929, p. 126 (A song of Owl Woman).

A FRAGMENT (Maya) (p. 48): From *The Magic World; American Indian Songs and Poems*, William Brandon, ed., Ohio Univ. Press, 1991, p. 5; Brandon's source: "A Hymn to the Creator and the Maker, the Mother and Father of Life," from the *Popul Vuh*, translated by Sylvanus Griswold Morley, Norman, Okla., 1950.

LOVE-CHARM SONG (Tupi) (p. 49): From *The Magic World; American Indian Songs and Poems*, William Brandon, ed., Ohio Univ. Press, 1991, p. 6; adapted from Couto de Magalães, *O Selvagem*, Rio de Janeiro, 1976. According to Brandon, the Amazonian Tupi were cannibals; however, he also quotes Spinden to the effect that their poetry was especially admired by the French dating from 1550 "when a large band of Tupi Indians took part in a festival at Rouen."

THE NORTH STAR (Osage) (p. 50): From *The Magic World; American Indian Songs and Poems*, William Brandon, ed., Ohio Univ. Press, 1991, p. 75; from Francis LaFlesche, "The Osage Tribe: Two Versions of the Child-Naming Rite," in *Forty-third BAE Report*, Washington, D.C., 1928.

TALL DOG TALE (Melecite) (p. 51): From *The Magic World; American Indian Songs and Poems*, William Brandon, ed., Ohio Univ. Press, 1991, p. 110; adapted from Frank G. Speck, "Malecite Tales," in *Journal of Amercan Folk-Lore*, Vol. 30, No. 198, 1917.

GUARDIAN SPIRIT SONG (Nez Percés) (p. 52): From *The Magic World; American Indian Songs and Poems*, William Brandon, ed., Ohio Univ. Press, 1991, p. 136; from Spinden, *Songs of the Tewa*, New York, 1933.

SPRING SONG (FRAGMENT) (Eskimo) (p. 53): From *The Magic World; American Indian Songs and Poems*, William Brandon, ed., Ohio Univ. Press, 1991, p. 140; from Knud Rasmussen, *The Intellectual Culture of the Iglulik Eskimos*, Copenhagen, 1929.

TEZOZOMOC, A SONG OF NEZALHUALCOYOTL (Nahuatl) (p. 54): From *The Magic World; American Indian Songs and Poems*, William Brandon, ed., Ohio Univ. Press, 1991, p. 24; adapted by Brandon from Daniel G. Brinton, *Ancient Nahuatl Poetry*, Philadelphia, 1887 (p. 20 in my copy). Nezahualcoyotl, a poet-king, is the best-known of the pre-Conquest Nahuatl-speaking poets of the Valley of Mexico. For comparison, Brinton's translation follows:

1. Listen with attention to the lamentations which I, the King Nezahualcoyotl, make upon my power, speaking with myself, and offering an example to others.

2. O restless and striving king, when the time of thy death shall come, thy subjects shall be destroyed and driven forth; they shall sink into dark oblivion. Then in thy hand shall no longer be the power and the rule, but with the Creator, the All-powerful.

3. He who saw the palaces and court of the old King Tezozomoc, how flourishing and powerful was his sway, may see them now dry and withered; it seemed as if they should last forever, but all that the world offers is illusion and deception, as everything must end and die.

4. Sad and strange it is to see and reflect on the prosperity and power of the old and dying King Tezozomoc; watered with ambition and avarice, he grew like a willow tree rising above the grass and flowers of spring, rejoicing for a long time, until at length, withered and decayed, the storm wind of death tore him from his roots, and dashed him in fragments to the ground. The same fate befell the ancient King Colzatzli, so that no memory was left of him, nor of his lineage.

5. In these lamentations and in this sad song, I now call to memory and offer as an example that which takes place in the spring, and the end

which overtook King Tezozomoc; and who, seeing this, can refrain from tears and wailing, that these various flowers and rich delights are bouquets that pass from hand to hand and all wither and end even in the present life!

6. Ye sons of kings and mighty lords, ponder well and think upon that which I tell you in these my lamentations, of what takes place in spring and of the end which overtook King Tezozomoc; and who, seeing this, can refrain from tears and wailing that these various flowers and rich delights are bouquets that pass from hand to hand and all wither and end even in the present life!

7. Let the birds now enjoy, with melodious voices, the abundance of the house of the flowery spring, and the butterflies sip the nectar of its flowers.

INTRODUCTION OF A CHILD (Omaha) (p. 56): From *The Sky Clears, Poetry of the American Indians*, A. Grove Day, ed., p. 104; attributed to Alice C. Fletcher and Francis LaFlesche, "The Omaha Tribe," 27th *Annual Report*, Bureau of American Ethnology, Washington, D.C., 1911, pp. 15-654.

THE ROCK (Omaha) (p. 58): From *The Magic World; American Indian Songs and Poems*, William Brandon, ed., Ohio Univ. Press, 1991, p. 83; adapted from Alice C. Fletcher and Francis LaFlesche, "The Omaha Tribe," in *Twenty-seventh Annual BAE Report*, Washington, D.C., 1911.

FROM THE AZTEC CALENDAR, THE FIRST MONTH (Nahuatl)(p. 59): A fragment from "From the Aztec Ceremonial Calendar," in *The Magic World; American Indian Songs and Poems*, William Brandon, ed., Ohio Univ. Press, 1991,

p. 9; adapted by Brandon from Book II of Fray Bernardino de Sahagun, *General History of the Things of New Spain;* the *Florentine Codex,* translated by Charles E. Dibble and Arthur J.O. Anderson, Santa Fe, 1950.

SONG OF LAMENTATION (Aztec) (p. 60): From *The Sky Clears, Poetry of the American Indians,* A. Grove Day, ed., p. 174; attributed to Daniel G. Brinton, *Ancient Nahuatl Poetry, Library of American Aboriginal Literature, Vol. 7,* Philadelphia, 1885. That this poem is titled in Brinton's translation,"By a Certain Ruler in Memory of Former Rulers," indicates that it was not intended as an apology for the child-sacrifices described in the preceding poem. Nevertheless, the juxtaposition is instructive.

SONG OF THE EARTH SPIRIT, ORIGIN LEGEND (Navajo) (p. 62): Vinson Brown, *Voices of Earth and Sky,* Stackpole Books, Harrisburg, Pennsylvania, 1974, p. 211; from *Navajo Wildlands,* Ballantine Books-Sierra Club, San Francisco, 1969, p. 124.

TWELFTH SONG OF THE THUNDER (Navajo) (p. 63): From *The Sky Clears, Poetry of the American Indians,* A. Grove Day, ed., p. 65; from Washington Matthews, "Navaho Myths, Prayers and Songs," P.E. Goddard, Ed., Univ. of Cal. *Publications* in American Archaeology and Ethnology, Vol. 5, No. 2, Berkeley, 1907.

FROM THE WIND CHANT (Navajo) (p. 64): From *The Magic World; American Indian Songs and Poems,* William Brandon, ed., Ohio Univ. Press, 1991,

p. 64; freely adapted by Brandon from "*Nilth Chiji Bakaji*" (Wind Chant), told by Hasteen Klah, retold in shorter form by Mary C. Wheelwright in *Bulletin No. 4, Museum of Navajo Ceremonial Art*, Sante Fe, 1946.

LOVE CHARM SONG (Chippewa) (p. 65): From *The Sky Clears, Poetry of the American Indians*, A. Grove Day, ed., p. 152; from Densmore, "Chippewa Music," *Bulletin 45*, Bureau of American Ethnology, Washington, D.C., 1910; a different version of this poem appear in *The Magic World; American Indian Songs and Poems*, William Brandon, ed., Ohio Univ. Press, 1991, p. 99.

FROM THE AZTEC CALENDAR, THE SEVENTH MONTH (Nahuatl) (p. 66): A fragment from "From the Aztec Ceremonial Calendar," in *The Magic World; American Indian Songs and Poems*, William Brandon, ed., Ohio Univ. Press, 1991, p. 9; adapted by Brandon from Book II of Fray Bernardino de Sahagun, *General History of the Things of New Spain*, the *Florentine Codex*, translated by Charles E. Dibble and Arthur J.O. Anderson, Santa Fe, 1950.

AZTEC SONG (Nahuatl) (p. 67): From *The Magic World; American Indian Songs and Poems*, William Brandon, ed., Ohio Univ. Press, 1991, p. 4; from Antonio Peñafiel, *MS Colección de Cantares Mexicanos, National Library of Mexico, Folio 17*; reprinted from *The Aztecs: People of the Sun*, by Alfonso Caso, translated by Lowell Dunham, Univ. of Oklahoma Press, 1958.

MAGPIE SONG (Navajo) (p. 68): From *The Sky Clears, Poetry of the American Indians*, A. Grove Day, ed., p. 96; attributed to Washington Matthews, "Navaho Gambling Songs," *American Anthropologist*, Vol. 2, No. 1 (O.S.), 1889, pp. 1-20.

OFFERING (Zuñi) (p. 69): From *In the Trail of the Wind, American Indian Poems and Ritual Orations*, John Bierhorst, ed., p. 108; translated from the Zuñi by Ruth Bunzel, in her "Introduction to Zuñi Ceremonialism," *Bureau of American Ethnology, 47th Annual Report*, 1929-30, pp. 483-4.

A SONG OF NEZALHUALCOYOTL (Nahuatl) (p. 70): From *The Sky Clears, Poetry of the American Indians*, A. Grove Day, ed., p. 180; from Daniel G. Brinton, *Ancient Nahuatl Poetry*, Library of American Aboriginal Literature, Vol. 6, Philadelphia, 1887.

HEAR MY VOICE (Cherokee) (p. 73): From *The Sky Clears, Poetry of the American Indians*, A. Grove Day, ed., p. 155; attributed to Henry Rowe Schoolcraft, *Historical and Statistical Information Respecting the History, Condition, and Prospects of the Indian Tribes of the Untied States*, 6 vols., Philadelphia, 1851-1857.

OMEN (Aztec) (p. 74): From *In the Trail of the Wind, American Indian Poems and Ritual Orations*, John Bierhorst, ed., p. 138; translated from the Aztec by Bernardino de Sahagún, in his *Historia General de las Cosas de Nueva España*, Libro 12, capítulo 1.

COYOTE TALE (Hopi) (p. 75): From *The Magic World; American Indian Songs and Poems*, William Brandon, ed., Ohio Univ. Press, 1991, p. 44; adapted by Brandon from Matilda Coxe Stevenson, "The Zuñi Indians," *Twenty-third Annual BAE Report*, Washington, D.C., 1904.

YOU SAY (SMOHALLA) (Nez Percés) (p. 78): Adapted from *American Indian Prose and Poetry*, Margot Astrov, ed., Capricorn Books, New York, 1962, p. 85; attributed to Herbert J. Spinden, *The Nez Percés Indians*, p. 261, and B. Alexander, *Mythology of North America*, p. 150. (According to Astrov, Somalla, from whose oration this poem is adapted, founded the Dreamer Religion based on traditional tribal beliefs, in response to the early embrace of Christianity by the Nez Percés.)

PRAYER FOR THE DAY (Nootka) (p. 79): From *American Indian Prose and Poetry*, Margot Astrov, ed., Capricorn Books, New York, 1962, p. 279; attributed to Frances Densmore, *Nootka and Quileute Music*, p. 285.

*　　*　　*

www.ingramcontent.com/pod-product-compliance
Lightning Source LLC
Chambersburg PA
CBHW021202020426
42331CB00003B/174

9 780578 013763